Bedtime Stories for Toddlers

A Collection of Bedtime Stories to Let Your Kids Sleep Tight

Imogen Young

© Copyright 2021 - All rights reserved.

The content contained within this book may not be reproduced, duplicated or transmitted without direct written permission from the author or the publisher.
Under no circumstances will any blame or legal responsibility be held against the publisher, or author, for any damages, reparation, or monetary loss due to the information contained within this book. Either directly or indirectly.

Legal Notice:
This book is copyright protected. This book is only for personal use. You cannot amend, distribute, sell, use, quote or paraphrase any part, or the content within this book, without the consent of the author or publisher.

Disclaimer Notice:
Please note the information contained within this document is for educational and entertainment purposes only. All effort has been executed to present accurate, up to date, and reliable, complete information. No warranties of any kind are declared or implied. Readers acknowledge that the author is not engaging in the rendering of legal, financial, medical or professional advice. The content within this book has been derived from various sources. Please consult a licensed professional before attempting any techniques outlined in this book.

By reading this document, the reader agrees that under no circumstances is the author responsible for any losses, direct or indirect, which are incurred as a result of the use of information contained within this document, including, but not limited to, — errors, omissions, or inaccuracies.

Table of Contents

Sidney	6
The Frog Tells the Truth	13
The Big Day	20
The Vervet Monkey	26
It's ok don't cry	33
Deanna Dragon Does Chores	46
The Emu	53
The Lumbermen	61
Swinging into the Sky	67
Tyrannosaurus	74
The Buffaloes	82
The Magician	87
The Great Unicorn Hunter	94
Ilongoria	101

Sidney

"It's time to get up Sidney," Mom called. The day is almost half over

"I'm sleepy mom, I'll get up soon," Sidney replied

Sidney was a lazy and sleepy sloth who loved to sleep more than anything else. She enjoyed laying the trees with the sun warming her and sleeping. Sloths are not very busy animals but Sidney knew there was not much to do today so she wanted to sleep all day.

"Hey Sidney, Want to go with me and pick leaves?" Becky Sloth called out to Sidney.

"No... I'm a sleepy sloth" Sidney slurred her words because she was so sleepy.

"Ok, you're going to miss out on all the fun," Becky said and she headed off to pick leaves

Sidney fell back to sleep right away. A few hours later Sidney's dad came by and tried to wake her up.

"Sidney it's time to do your chores, come on let's go," Dad instructed

Sidney rolled over and dragged herself around doing her chores but she kept falling asleep. At one time she fell asleep on the vacuum and it sucked all the dirt off on only one section of the floor.

"Sidney!" Mom yelled, "Wake up honey you are sleeping on the vacuum."

"Oh, ok mom sorry," Sidney said with a sleepy voice. She walked back to the branch and fell back to sleep.

The next day her mother was throwing a party and they had invited a lot of the jungle animals. It was going to be the party of the season. Sidney's mother had been planning for months for this party and she wanted everything to be perfect.

"Sidney I'm going to need your help today." Mom tried to encourage Sidney

"Ok mom I'll help," Sidney said as she got up and went to help. Sidney helped the kitchen make the food and it was her job to put the food on trays so someone else could take it out to the guests. Sidney tried to stay awake but her eyes just didn't want to stay open. Soon she was fast asleep on one of the trays.

"Sidney...Sidney. Wake up!" One of the guests said. "Your mom would like the snacks put out. Are you ok?"

"I'm so sleepy. Tell mom I can't help anymore" Sidney slowly walked out and went back to her branc h

The party continued but there was no food put out for anyone. Mom looked around and didn't see Sidney anywhere and felt sad that the guests were not getting the food she had put together for everyone. Soon the party ended and everyone started to head back to their houses. Mom thanked everyone for coming and apologized about the food. Just as the last guest left and mom closed the door Sidney came into the room.

"Hi mom, I am all rested now can we do something?" Sidney said with wide-awake eyes.

"Sidney all of my guests have left. The party is over. You fell asleep in the kitchen and none of the food got put out. What am I going to do with all of this leftover food? Sidney I was counting on you to help me. I am very disappointed." Mom said as she left the room.

Sidney stood there feeling sad that she had let her mom down. There was so much food left that had to be eaten. Sidney thought about it for a moment and then she had a great idea. She would throw a surprise party for her mom the next day and stay awake and serve the food. This would show her mom that she didn't mean to let her down. She hurried as best she could and invited everyone back for a second celebration.

Everyone showed up while her mom was out gathering things from the jungle. When she returned, she thought it was odd that the lights were all off. Mom walked into the room and the lights popped on and everyone jumped out

"SURPRISE!" everyone yelled

"Oh my goodness," Mom said surprised, "what is going on?"

Sidney stepped forward and said, "Mom I felt bad that I didn't help you the other day so I wanted to surprise you with a party that you didn't have to plan or work at. I want you to enjoy the party and I will take care of everything."

Her mother was so happy that she cried with happiness. For hours her mother talked to the guests and they all enjoyed the food that had been prepared. Sidney worked hard to make sure that all the food was placed out and that everyone had plenty to eat and drink. When the party was winding down Mom came over and gave Sidney a big hug.

"Sidney I was so sad yesterday when you didn't help me but today, I am overjoyed that you have stepped up and reorganized the party and that you are doing what you can to help me enjoy the day with my friends." Mom cheerfully stated

Sidney felt good that she was able to undo the mess she had created the day before and she indicated that she would do her best to try to only sleep at night and help out more during the day so her mom didn't have to do so much.

The Frog Tells the Truth

Terrance sat on a tree limb watching the other tree frogs talk about things they heard or did at the lily pad pond earlier. Everyone was talking about the big news.

"Have you heard," One frog said, "There are going to be turtles let loose in our pond."

"That's not what I heard." Another croaked, "I heard that they are going to drain our pond to make it a parking lot."

At this point, all the frogs had begun to croak about what they had heard and thought was going to happen to the Lily pad pond. But Terrance just sat and listened. He didn't want to say anything that was not true but didn't want the other frogs spreading stories about what may or may not happen either.

So Terrance decided to go find out what was going to happen. He leaped on the log floating down the stream toward the big building where all the people worked.

These people helped all kinds of animals and Terrance thought they would know what was going on.

He stuck himself to one of the windows and tried to listen to what they were saying. He couldn't hear anything. He hopped over by the door and waited for it to open then he snuck in. He landed on a plant that was in the corner of a big room. There were many people around a table talking about the lily pad pond. They talked about a lot of different things and Terrance got confused about what might happen.

"The pond has been there for a long time." One person said. "We need to consider all of the fish and frogs that live there."

"Yes, we have taken all of that into consideration and we will make sure everything is still ok" the man in the suit said at the other end of the table.

Terrance had heard enough and he snuck back out of the building and floated back to the lily pad pond where he waited for all of the other frogs to come that evening so he could share what he had heard. Finally, they started coming one by one and after a short while the pond was full of croaking frogs.

"Terrance, you have news for us about the pond?" the head tree frog asked

"I do but I don't have all the information just yet. I want to let you all now that the information I have said that the frogs and fish will all be safe. I do not know what to tell you now but I wanted to tell you the truth so we all didn't get scared. I will let you all know when I have more information."

The other frogs seemed relieved that Terrence had taken the time to seek out the truth so they all could rest easy.

The next day there were some big trucks by the lily pad pond and they were testing the water and taking dirt samples out of the ground.

"This should be enough for us to test and prove our case. The pond did need attention." One of the workers mentioned

"Need attention?" Terrance thought what did that mean. He hopped on the back of the truck and hid behind some tools. He listened and tried to see what was going on.

"Water seems good." One worker said .

" The soil appears to be good as well." The other added. "I don't see any issues here" the men got into their truck. Terrence hopped off and went back to the lily pad pond.

There was a lot of commotion at the pond this afternoon. Someone had said that the pond was contaminated and that is why they were testing the water.

Terrence piped up, "The water is NOT contaminated. I was there today when they tested the water and the dirt. They said everything was fine!"

The other frogs felt relieved and again were happy that Terrance was telling them the truth.

A few days later a large truck backed up the pond. All of the frogs stopped croaking and sat quietly as they watched. Terrence quickly hopped over to the truck. Inside were many tiny fish and frogs. They were bringing them to the lily pad pond because the water is so good and there was room for more animals. Terrence tried to hear why they were bringing them to the pond and he heard one of the men say that these fish and frogs needed a safe place. They had been living in a small pond near a garbage dump and it was not safe.

The other frogs began to croak and tell stories. But Terrance called a meeting and shared what he had heard with the other frogs .

"We need to welcome these fish and frogs. They need a safe place to live. They are not going to run us out of the pond and we can live together." Terrance tried to convince the other frogs that were already from the pond.

"Tell us the truth Terrance!" the frogs begged, "will there be enough room for all of us to live here together?"

All of the frogs knew Terrance always told the truth so they could count on his word.

"I have heard them say that it will be safe here and that we can all live happily. Having the new frogs and fish here will be better for us all." Terrance spoke the truth as he had heard it firsthand. The frogs croaked quietly and then one of them jumped forward.

"Terrance, we want you to be in charge of the pond. You always tell the truth and we can trust you. Will you be the Frog in charge?" they cheered.

Terrance replied, "If we all tell the truth we can all be trusted and we can all live happily." The frogs thought that was a good idea and they all agreed to not talk about things that they were not sure about. They only wanted to tell the truth.

The Big Day

Today was the big day of Una Unicorn. She was going to have her very first dance recital. She had been practicing all year for this day. She had memorized each step, every twirl and every leap in the routine. She was ready to dance.

Una started getting ready to go. She got her mane brushed and put ribbons in it. She shined up her horn and put on her favorite cape for the performance. She put her dance music in her bag and they headed off to the Recital. Una couldn't wait to show off her moves and surprise the judges with what she had prepared.

When they arrived at the recital location Una hugged her parents and they wished her good luck.

"You have worked so hard to get ready for this and we are so proud of you. If you do your best and do what you practiced you will do wonderful." Mom encouraged Una.

Una headed backstage to make the final preparations. She practiced her routine one more time, brushed her hair and made sure her costume was perfect. When it was her turn, she patiently waited for her name to be called onto the stage.

Right when she thought it was her turn the director of the recital whispered to the stage manager and they came off and told they needed to let another dancer go before Una. Una was shocked and upset.

"But it's my turn," Una said confused

"Yes but there has been a change in the schedule and this is what we need to do" The stage manager indicated.

Una stomped her hoof and pouted. She walked back to the waiting area and waited.

The other dancer took the stage and as it turned out the music, she used the same music of Una. Una was in shock and started to get more upset. What was she going to do? The music was the same. How could the judges look at her dance different if the music was the same? Una began to worry.

The other dancer finished her routine and the audience applauded. The recital director entered the stage and announced Una's name. Una didn't want to go on next. She was afraid the judges would see her dance as the same since the music was the same. The more she thought about it the more upset she got.

She stepped out on the stage and tried to ask if she could wait but the director didn't listen to her. Her music started and Una took her spot. But she had forgotten how her dance started. She had gotten so upset that she forgot how her dance started. She tried to think fast and remember her moves.

The music stopped.

"Are you ok Una?" the Judge called out.

"I think so. I just couldn't remember how my dance started. I have the same music and I want to make sure my dance is unique." Una tried to explain.

The judges looked at one another and replied, "Every dancer is unique even if the music is the same. We are happy to restart your music if you are ready to continue."

"Yes please, I'd like to restart" Una agreed. She stood there and took a big breath. She closed her eyes and started thinking about her routine and once she calmed down it took no time at all for her routine to come back to her mind and she was ready to go.

Her music began and Una started dancing. She remembered every move, twirl and jump that she had practiced for many months earlier. Her routine finished and Una took a bow. The audience applauded for her and she walked off the stage to wait and see how the judges scored her routine.

Una and the other dancers waited off stage for the results. Then the judges started calling out the dancers by name. Una's name was called out at the runner up. She won a ribbon for 2nd place. At first, she was disappointed. She thought about her routine and what she may have done wrong and when she took the stage the judges congratulated her on a perfect performance. They said she had a wonderful form and a great routine. They scored her down only because she needed to restart the music. Una thanked the judges and accepted her award.

On the way home, she looked at her ribbon and although she was proud that she did her best she knew that if she had not gotten so upset about having to wait her turn, she wouldn't have had to restart the music and maybe she would have won.

She learned a good lesson that day about not letting things get you upset. Sometimes things happen and they are things you cannot change. You can choose to get upset and maybe forget your dance routine or take a deep breath and do your best.

The Vervet Monkey

It was lunchtime and that was Vanessa's favorite time of the day. She loved eating her yummy fruits and nuts.

Today at lunch there was a new student. They had just moved to this area and the new girl, Sue, had just arrived at the school and didn't know she needed to bring her lunch. On the first day, no one talked to Sue and she sat by herself. After lunch finished all the monkeys went back to class and Sue was in Vanessa's class too .

"Students we have a new member in our classroom." The teacher announced.

Everyone looked up to the front to see Sue. "Please make her feel welcome. Sue, you can sit over by Wilber and Vanessa." Wilbur and Vanessa raised their hands so sue knew where to go.

At the last break in the day, Vanessa had a chance to go talk to Sue and introduce herself.

"Hello, my name is Vanessa. I'm a Vervet Monkey and I have lived here all my life." Vanessa said proudly.

"Hello, my name is Sue. I'm just a regular monkey?" Sue said shyly. " We just moved here. I don't know anyone." Sue said as she rubbed her toe into the ground

"Everyone here is super nice," Vanessa smiled and continued, "We all play together after school too, if you want to you can come."

"That would be great. We are still moving today but maybe we can play tomorrow?" Sue asked

"Sure thing!" Vanessa confirmed .

The next day was Saturday and all the kids played at the jungle gym. Vanessa watched for Sue and waited for her to come. Soon Sue came along swinging through the trees.

"There she is!" Vanessa yelled out. "Over here, Sue!' Vanessa waved her arms.

Sue saw all the other monkeys playing on the Jungle Gym and was excited to join in. She laughed and climbed all over the trees with Vanessa. They had a great time. Soon lunchtime rolled around and all the monkeys got their lunches out to sit and eat.

"Sue, did you bring your lunch?" Vanessa Asked

"No, I didn't know I needed to bring one today," Sue replied

"Oh that's ok I have lots of food. We can share." Vanessa offered with a smile

The two girls sat and ate Vanessa's lunch and lay in the sun for a while.

"Thanks for sharing your lunch, Vanessa. That was very nice of you." Sue thanked her with a hug.

"Anytime Friend" Vanessa hugged her back .

They ran off back to the Jungle gym and played with all the other monkeys. After lunch, all the monkeys were climbing all over the trees, running and jumping from vine to vine and they even began to swing from their tails. Sue was having the time of her life.

She made lots of new friends. When the day was over the sky was getting dark and all the monkeys started to head home. Sue couldn't wait for the next school day to come to hang out with Vanessa and the other monkeys.

Monday morning came and Vanessa swung by Sues house so they could go to school together.

"Good morning Vanessa." Sues mother said. "Thank you so much for letting sue play this weekend and sharing your lunch."

"Sue is so great and I am glad you moved here. She is my friend and friends share." Vanessa replied. The girls headed off to school talking about the funny things from the weekend and what they wanted to do the next weekend.

School started and all the monkeys sat in their seats and started to learn. They learned about science and math in the morning. Vanessa didn't care for math but Sue loved it. And Sue didn't like Science but Vanessa loved it so they could help each other out. Soon it was time for lunch .

All the monkeys scurried out to the lunchroom to get their lunches and start eating. Sue grabbed her lunch sack and went to find Vanessa. Vanessa was sitting on the floor in the classroom crying.

"I forgot my lunch on the counter at home." She cried. "I was so excited to come at school that I forgot it."

Sue felt bad that Vanessa forgot her food but she had a great idea.

"Vanessa, don't worry. Friends Share remember!" Sue reminded Vanessa about Saturday and how they had shared Vanessa's lunch because Sue did not have one.

"Are you sure you don't mind sharing?" Vanessa asked

"Of course not I have more than enough," Sur reassured Vanessa

The two girls ran off to the lunchroom to sit and share Sue's lunch.

"I'm glad friends share," Vanessa said to Sue

"Me Too" Sue replied with a big smile

It's ok don't cry

"There is a bee on my arm and it stung me!" Whitney cried out. "Help me!"

Whitney's mother came running outside to see if she was ok.

"I'm just joking. There was no Bee mom." Whitney laughed

"Whitney that was not funny. If you keep telling stories like that when there is a real emergency no one will believe you. That is called a crying wolf. You need to be very careful" Mother Warthog scolded.

Whitney laughed and trotted off down the road. Along the way, she visited her friend who lived at the farm. They had a lot of really fun things to do there. They could run in the field as fast as they could. They could chase the chickens. They could swing in the swing and they could splash in the creek. Whitney loved visiting there.

On her way home Whitney stopped by the park. She saw some older warthogs playing and thought she would play a trick on them. She climbed up on the highest part of the playground equipment and began to cry out .

"Help me I am up too high and I am scared to get down!" Whitney faked a cry and watched as the other warthogs came over to see what was going on.

"It's ok don't cry," one of them said to her. "We can help you get down here come this way."

Whitney jumped off the equipment and yelled "Tricked you! I am not scared to be up there."

"We came over here to help you and you didn't need help?" One of the girls questioned. "We will know better next time. If you cry out for help, we won't help you if you are just going to play jokes.

Whitney lumped in circles laughing because she had tricked the older warthogs. They just walked away from her grumbling at her not-so-funny joke.

Whitney continued on her way home. She found some other warthogs playing along the way. She thought it would be a good idea to trick them. So she started to limp like her leg was hurt.

"My leg is hurt. I need help" Whitney said with a shaky voice. " Can you help me?"

The other warthogs came rushing over to help.

"I can carry you on my back if that helps your leg?" One of the warthogs offered.

"I have a wagon we can tow you to home in it." Another one added. "What can we do to help you?"

Whitney stood there looking sad then Jumped up laughing. "Jokes on you, I don't need help I'm fine."

The other warthogs got upset at Whitney for joking them and they ran off .

It was getting very dark outside and it was taking longer than Whitney thought to arrive at home. "I must have gone the wrong way?" Whitney thought to herself.

She had gone home from the park many times and never gotten lost.

Her mother began to call for her and Whitney heard her. She began running toward her mom's voice and when she got home, she felt relieved.

"I thought I was lost," Whitney said breathing heavy from running

" Well, I don't believe that Whitney. You know the way home." Mother Warthog said as she looked at Whitney with a frown.

When the sun came up Whitney headed off to the farm again. It was a rainy day which made running in the dirt extra fun. There was the mud and that was a fun sticky mess.

Whitney and her friend played all day and then more rain came making it stickier and muddier.

"We need to be careful not to get stuck in the mud Whitney," her friend warned. It's hard to get out of the mud out here .

The girls ran and played slipping and sliding around. They started to chase the chickens again and as they rounded the corner to the big red barn Whitney slipped and fell into a big mud pit. She laughed at first then realized that it was too sticky for her to get out all by herself. She tried to pull her legs out of the mud but they seemed to be stuck like glue. Every time she tried to pull them up, it sucked them in more and more. She knew she was in big trouble.

"Hello Can someone come help me please! I am stuck in the mud," Whitney cried out. No one came. She yelled louder, "HELP ME I am stuck in the mud!"

What was she going to do? No one was coming to help her. She looked around for a while to see if there was something, she could use to pull herself out but she couldn't reach anything. Just then the older warthogs from the park were walking by. At last Whitney could get some help.

"Hi guys can you help me? I am stuck in the mud and I cannot get out." Whitney asked.

"Are you kidding? We are not going to fall for that trick again" They laughed and kept walking.

Whitney signed and tried to free herself again. No luck, she was stuck.

She saw the other warthogs she tricked and asked if they would help her but they said, "No, you are probably joking us again."

Whitney began to regret all the jokes she had played on the other warthogs because no one would help her. She was stuck for a long time and her friend finally came around the corner.

"There you are silly. What are you doing in the mud?" she asked

"Oh man am I glad to see you. I am stuck. I mean stuck." Whitney tried to explain

"Whitney you are always joking. That's not funny. Being stuck can be very dangerous. You need to get out of there." Her friend said and she walked away

"Wait! Come back, please. This is for REAL! I AM STUCK!" Whitney shouted louder than ever before. Her friend peeked back around the corner "Please help me this is for real. Whitney pleaded.

Her friend saw that Whitey was in real trouble and ran to get help. She had a hard time convincing people to come but finally, she got Whitney's mom and another warthog at the farm to help.

"I am so glad to see all of you I have been stuck here almost all afternoon and no one would help me," Whitney whined.

"We are here now but it's no surprise no one came to help you. You like to play tricks on people all the time so they don't believe you. I warned you about crying wolf." Mother Warthog scolded.

It took 3 warthogs, a rope and 2 shovels to dig Whitney out of the mud. When she was out, she was grateful and hugged everyone that helped.

"I am so sorry that I played tricks on you before. I can now see how joking around being hurt or stuck was a bad thing to do." Whitney seemed to see how her jokes had made stay stuck in the mud all afternoon.

"No more crying wolf?" Mother Asked

"No more crying wolf. I promise." Whitney said

Yanny the Yak is Brave

"Are you sure you want to go in there?" Yanny asked his friend Walt.

"I'm not afraid to go in there, it's not that dark," Walt replied.

Yanny was afraid of a lot of things and the dark was a big one. He didn't go into a room unless the light is on or there is a night light. Yanny and Walt played in the basement of Yanny's house and the storage room had the light burned out. The boys wanted to go there because there was a box of toys they wanted to play with.

"Come on, Walt, let's go we don't need those toys," Yanny said as he walked up the stairs. Walt turned around and the boys went up the stairs. They went outside to play instead.

Besides the dark Yanny didn't like to be home alone. He was too old for a babysitter but didn't think he was ready to be left home alone. Yanny's mom had recently decided to go back to work to mean Yanny would need to come home after school for a few hours and stay by himself.

"Yanny tomorrow is the first day you will be home after school by yourself. Do you have any questions?" Yanny's mom aske d

"I think so, I mean I would rather go to Walt 's house but he has a dentist appointment tomorrow and won't be there," Yanny replied to his mother

"You will be fine," his mother reassured him. "I have left a list of phone numbers if you need them, there are snacks for after school, and I will be home 2 hours after you get here."

The next morning came and Yanny got ready for school. He went over the list of numbers and made sure he knew where everything was if he needed it. He checked to see where the snacks were and he made sure that he had his mom's new work number in his pocket. When he headed out the door his mom hugged him and smiled.

"Yanny, you are so brave and I am so proud of you. You are growing up so fast. She told him

"I don't know mom, I don't know if I am ready to be home alone," Yannyn replied

"I wouldn't leave you here if you were not ready, trust me," Mom and she walked him out the door. "Have a GREAT day and I'll see you when I get home."

The school bell rang and the students headed home for the day. Yanny headed right home and locked the door behind himself when he got home. He checked where the phone numbers were again and made sure that his mom's phone number was right by the phone. He sat at the table, had a snack, and waited for his mom to come home.

Ring Ring...The phone rang and Yanny ran to answer it.

"Hello?" Yanny answered

"Hi Yanny its mom," Mom replied. "You doing ok? I'll be home soon ok?"

"Yes, I'm ok mom. I have had my snack and the doors are locked and I have all the phone numbers you left me here on the counter." Yanny reassured her

"That's good, I'll see you soon. Have a good afternoon." Mom ended the call.

Yanny hung up and went to sit and watch TV until she came home. He watched for a little while and then decided to play with some toys. But the toy he wanted was in the basement in the storage room. Yanny opened up the basement door and stood there looking down the stairs. He walked down to the door of the storage room and waited. Yanny didn't like the dark and the light switch was on the wall on the other side so he would have to walk into the dark to turn it on. He thought about whether he wanted that particular toy or not and he agreed he did. So he took a deep breath and stepped into the darkness .

"I can do this," He said to himself. "I am a big boy and I am brave."

He reached out and turned on the light. When the light filled the room he smiled.

"I knew I could do it!" Yanny said proudly. He found the toy he wanted and walked upstairs. As he reached the top of the basement stairs his mother was walking in the door from work.

"Yanny what are you doing in the basement?" She asked

"Mom, you won't believe it! I wanted to play with my toy and it was in the storage room, In the dark. But I am a big boy that stays home by himself now so I went down to get my toy. I turned on the light and got what I needed," He told her with a big smile

"Oh Yanny, That's great, I am so proud of you. You are very brave," his mother replied happily.

From tha t day on, Yanny stayed home after school by himself every day and was not afraid of the dark anymore.

Deanna Dragon Does Chores

"Deanna" Aunt Jenny called from the basement, "Can you please come down here?"

"I am playing video games on my phone, I'll be right down," Deanna yelled back

It was normal for Deanna to be playing games on her phone. She LOVED her phone. She loved her phone so much that she never put it down. She used it to play games, watch videos, listen to music and talk to friends and family. Deanna hardly ever put her phone down.

As she leaped down the stairs to see what her Aunt Jenny wanted, she stopped because a very funny video about kittens came on her phone. Deanna laughed and rolled on her back it was so funny. Those kittens jumping out of boxes made her laugh a long time.

"Deanna!" Aunt Jenny called again, "Come Here Now Please."

"I am really busy Aunt Jenny, can I come later?" Deanna said with a whine in her voice .

"I have some chores for you to do. We need to get them done so we can go to the park and play." Aunt Jenny replied.

Deanna sat on the stairs thinking about if she even really wanted to go to the park. She didn't want to do chores but she did want to go to the park. But if she didn't do the chores today maybe someone else would do them and she could go to the park tomorrow.

"MMMM- I don't want to go to the Park, Aunt Jenny. Thank you anyway." Danna said as she slid back up the stairs. She closed the door of her room and climbed into her blanket cave and watched more of those funny kitten videos.

A couple of hours later Deanna came downstairs for lunch. She looked around for everyone and couldn't find them. She scratched her head, "I wonder where everyone is?" Deanna turned and saw a note on the counter from her aunt Jenny.

'Deanna, we all got our chores done and went to the park for lunch and play. We will be back later for dinner. Love Aunt Jenny'

"Well that wasn't very nice," Deanna thought out loud "They just left me here...I did want to go to the park." Deanna sighed as she thought about not playing with her friends at the park .

Deanna looked around at the chores she was supposed to do thinking maybe someone did them for her. She ran to the basement excitedly hoping the laundry was folded. But when she arrived, she saw it was still sitting in a pile waiting for her. "Bleh," she mumbled.

"WAIT! Maybe the bathroom was cleaned." She ran up the stairs to the see if someone had cleaned the bathroom for her- after all, she HATED cleaning the bathroom.

"AHHHHH, WHHHyyy!" she yelled as she saw that the bathroom was just as she had left it. Wet towel on the floor, brush on the counter, and toothbrush in the sink; No one had cleaned up her mess after all. She looked like she was going to have to do the chores anyway.

Deanna was sad for missing out the trip to the park and she sat at the top of the stairs. If she just would have done her chores and not been so distracted by her phone, she could be having fun at the park. She flopped back and lay at the top of the stairs for a while. She fell asleep and started to dream about the fun things to do at the park: swinging, jumping rope, playing hide and seek or even eating her very favorite chocolate and peanut-butter flavored ice cream from the ice cream stand.

Ping! Deanna's phone chimed. Ping, ping, ping....her Aunt Jenny was sending her photos of the fun time they were having at the pa rk and that they were thinking about getting some ice cream later.

Deanna jumped up and ran to the bathroom. She cleaned up the toothbrush in the sink, put her hairbrush away, picked up her dirty towel and took it to the basement laundry area. She dumped out the clean basket of clothes and began to fold them. She took them up to her room and put them all away. She even took out the broom and swept the kitchen, hallway and dining room then mopped them for Aunt Jenny.

When she was done, she looked around to see if there was anything she had missed. Everything looked good and she reached for her phone to see if there was still time to meet everyone at the park. Just then Aunt Jenny walked in the front door. Deanna's head drooped. She had missed out on the park and ice cream.

"Hi Aunt Jenny, Are you guys done at the park?" Deanna said softly

"Deanna I just came home to get something and was going to go back." Aunt Jenny looked around, "Wow Deanna you did your chores. I appreciate that, and ....you swept and mopped up the floors too? That is a BIG help to me. Now I have time to make a cake for your class party tomorrow." Aunt Jenny said with excitement.

"Chocolate cake with peanut butter frosting?" Deanna piped up .

"I can do that, I have time now because you helped me do chores," Aunt Jenny said.

"I did want to go to the park Aunt Jenny, I am sorry, I didn't do my chores when you asked me to. I will try to not be on my phone so much and help out more." Deanna said with a smile

"That would be great Deanna, there is so much going on and so much fun stuff to do that I would hate for you to miss out on. And besides, because you helped me do chores can make your extra special favorite cake for tomorrow!"

Aunt Jenny put arm around Deanna and winked. "But for now, we can go to the park and enjoy the afternoon. Still want to come Deanna?" Aunt Jenny asked

"I sure do, let's go," Deanna said as she dashed out the door.

Because Deanna did her chores and helped Aunt Jenny with some extra chores Deanna got to take her very favorite extra special cake to school the next day.

The Emu

"I know!" Exclaimed Edmond when his teacher told him about the upcoming field trip his class was going to take. "I know all about the zoo. I have been there before."

"That's great Edmond but we have lots of students who have never been, so let's make sure we all have the opportunity to enjoy the zoo." Edmond's teacher said with a smile

Edmond's 3rd grade class was learning about the local zoo and what kind of animals were there and how the zoo takes care of the animals. They were planning a field trip next Tuesday and each student needed to learn about an animal that they liked.

"What animal did you pick Edmond?" his friend Suzy asked

"I already know everything about every animal at the zoo so I don't need to pick one." Edmond snapped at Suzy.

Suzy looked at Edmond with wide eyes and said, "Every animal? Wow, that's a lot." Suzy walked away.

The Monday before the field trip the students were giving their reports on their favorite animal. There were reports on Lions, Penguins, Turtles and even Porcupines. Edmond was called to the front of the room to give his report. He walked confidently to the front and stood there ready to give his report- about ALL of the animals.

"I have visited the zoo about a hundred times and I know all about all the animals there. I know all about what they eat and how they sleep and where all of the animals come from so, I don't need to report on just ONE animal." Edmond sounded like a Know it all and the other students chuckled.

"Edmond," the teacher interrupted, "Do you have a favorite animal at the zoo? One you like better than any other?"

"Nope, I know everything about all of them so I like them all the same!" Edmond replied.

Edmond took his seat feeling good about all the information he thought he knew. "Aaaand, I know everything about the zoo too, I know where to go in the zoo, where all the food and bathrooms are and I know the way to each of the animals so I can give directions to everyone," Edmond said before taking his seat.

His teacher smiled and shook her head, "Thank you, Edmond, let's see who else has a report to give." She moved on to another student.

Tuesday Morning came and Edmond was up early and ready to go. He shared tidbits of information with his mother, father, and brother before school and talked to the bus driver to school about how much he knew about the zoo. Everyone listened nicely but was happy when Edmond was finally at school.

As the student loaded the bus Edmond started in. "I know where to go when we get off the bus. I have been to the zoo…" Edmond was interrupted by another student

"...A hundred times, yes we know. You better stay with the group though we don't want to get lost. Not everyone has been to this zoo before."

Once at the zoo the students separated into groups with parents who came to help. Edmond was in the group of the teacher. They started in the lion's den and then they went to see the leopards.

"Ya know the next cage has a tiger in it!" Edmond said proudly with his arms crossed. "We need to go this way to see it."

The teacher guided the students along the path onto the next cage and sure enough, there were the Tigers. Edmond smirked.

As the students followed the path to the next group of animals there was a new sign showing that some of the animals had been moved and that an old section of the zoo had been closed. Edmond didn't see the sign and as the class followed the new path Edmond insisted that the way to the next area was the old way. He didn't follow the class and headed off the way he thought was the right way. A little while later Edmond found himself alone and, in an area, where there were no animals and no classmates and no teacher anywhere. Edmond stood there looking around wondering where he was. Was he lost? Where was everyone?

The teacher noticed Edmond was not with the group and she alerted the zoo workers to help her look for Edmond. They looked but could not find Edmond. Everyone was getting worried about him and Edmond was worried he would never find his class again. A few hours passed and one of the zookeepers was checking the old area for some tools. He saw Edmond sitting alone looking worried.

"Hello, Can I help you Lil fella? You seem to be lost." The zookeeper inquired

"I am here on a field trip but I got lost. I thought I knew how to go but I ended up here and I don't know where I am anymore." Edmond sniffled.

"I think I know where your class is. I saw a group over by the snack shack. Let me call the other zoo worker and we can have the teacher come get you." The Zookeeper offered in a kind voice .

Soon Edmond's teacher came rushing over with another zoo worker, "Edmond, are you ok? Where did you go?" his teacher said in a panic.

"Well I thought I knew where to go and thought you were going the wrong way so I came the old way and got lost. It was scary and I couldn't find my way back." Edmond said with a shaky voice.

"We are glad you are ok Edmond." His teacher reassured, "But it is important that you follow the directions of the person in charge so you don't get lost like today. We were all very scared."

"I am so sorry. I didn't mean to get lost." Edmond stood up and took the teacher's hand. "Maybe I don't know everything."

"None of us know everything all the time Edmond," the teacher said, "that's why we need to follow directions and stay with the group. Next time you think you know something different than a parent or teacher you should ask them. That way you can learn new ways to do things."

The class was excited to see Edmond and he was happy to be back with his class. The next day, the class talked about a new animal they learned about and when it was Edmond's turn, he stood up in front and said, "I know." Then he stopped and smiled. "I know that I learned I need to pay attention to my teacher and that I can learn new things if I don't think I know everything all the time."

Edmond and the other students laughed together and were happy that Edmond learned something new.

The Lumbermen

Once upon a time, there seemed to be a naughty little lamb which got in danger every day: - Oh, absolutely no! I am all smelly and dirty. Mummy will not be happy! - Said the concerned small lamb as he place inside a puddle of mud.

After some time his mum arrived, saw the little lamb, and got angry: - You won't ever tune in me, will you? How often have I told you never to go through such a height? - Said the mum of his, furiously.

- But, I also told you that it's fun. You don't listen to me either. - said the little lamb with confidence.

His mum couldn't hold a grudge and started laughing and hugging her son:

- Come now, let me clean you up. - said his mum with a smile.

T he little lamb´s mother was always worried about her son and always repeated:

- Be careful, my son! Do not go to the forest; wild animals live there. They could hurt you and even eat you. - warned his mother.

- You worry too much, Mummy. - said the little lamb, bravely.

Despite the warnings of his mother, the naughty little lamb often played in the forest till late in the evening.

One day, the little lamb went deep into the forest and found a beautiful spring:

- A spring! Just in time, I'm very thirsty. - said the little lamb, anxiously.

To calm his thirst, he decided to drink the water from the spring. While the little lamb drank, a scary wolf watched him from behind a tree:

- Ha, ha, ha! Today is my lucky day! I see a delicious and appetising little lamb. - said the hungry wolf.

Little by little, the wolf approached the lamb. As no one was there to save the poor little lamb the wolf said:

- Why are you drinking water from this wellspring? Don't you know that wild animals, like me, live in the forest? – said the wolf with an evil smile.

The little lamb was surprised to see the scary wolf. He knew that wolves could be dangerous.

- My mom warned me about the wolves and I'm sure that this ferocious animal wants to eat me for dinner. I need to run away as fast as I can! - thought the scared little lamb to himself.

- Apologies mighty, Mr. wolf. I'm just a little lamb who doesn't know much. - he said.

- You've also polluted the water. How can I drink it now? - Said the wolf.

- Forgive me again mighty, Mr. wolf, but on your side, the water is not polluted. The water flows from where you are standing, sir. – replied the little lamb, politely.

The wolf was amazed by the little lamb's intelligent response, but that did not change the fact that he just wanted to eat him.

- How dare you argue with me? I think you are the same little lamb that mistreated me last year! - said the wolf, furiously.

- But mighty Mr. wolf, I was not even born then. – said the frightened little lamb.

The little lamb realised that the wolf was trying to trick him so both the lamb and the wolf used words and gestures, wisely. Suddenly, from where he was standing, the little lamb saw some lumbermen coming towards him. He thought:

- If I keep talking to the wolf, I´ll buy some time for those lumbermen to come and chase the wolf away. - thought the little lamb to himself.

- Mighty Mr. wolf, you are right. I've polluted the water, but it wasn't my intention to make you angry. - said the little lamb, wisely.

- But, I'm already unsettled. - replied the wolf.

- Oh, let me make it up to you by telling you a story. – said the little lamb, pretending not to be scared of the wolf.

- A story? Argh, what a waste of time! But, I will listen and slowly get close to him so I don't have get tired chasing him around.– thought the wolf sneakily to himself.

- Once upon a time…. - started the little lamb.

By telling the story, the little lamb kept the wolf at bay while the lumbermen got closer until they saw them:

- Look! A wolf! They are so dangerous. - pointed out the lumbermen.

T he lumbermen stopped the wolf from eating the lamb. The little lamb was very relieved.

- Today I was very lucky; this could have ended in a very different way. That wolf could have eaten me. - thought the little lamb about the risk he had taken.

He quickly ran home to his mother to tell her what had happened in the forest with the wolf and the lumbermen. Then, he promised his mum that he would never go into the forest again and his mother felt relieved:

- Oh yes, mother, now I understand. I should never go again to dangerous places where fierce and wild animals could eat me.

Swinging into the Sky

Do you like to swing on the swing set? Have you ever swung yourself so high it felt like you could swing right into the sky? Well, guess what? You can swing right now without having to go anywhere near an actual swing set. You can- In your mind! Your mind is capable of doing many incredible things, including something called Visualization.

To begin your visualization practice, close your eyes. Close your eyes (unless you are the one reading this, of course!) To build a very strong visualization, it is usually helpful to first center yourself and be sure you are giving your brain the very best tools it needs to work with. In this case, that means oxygen, and oxygen means taking some good, deep breaths.

You are going to take some slow, deep breaths now, following my instruction: Breathe in very slowly, 1 – 2 – 3 – 4. Now breathe out, very slowly, 1 – 2 – 3 – 4. Excellent. Now again very slowly, 1 – 2 – 3 – 4 and breathe back out very slowly, 1 – 2 – 3 – 4 very nice.

Once more, very slowly in 1 – 2 – 3 – 4 and back out very slowly, 1 – 2 – 3 – 4. Great!

Take a moment to review how you feel. Are you comfy and feeling good? Okay, great.

See yourself in your mind now. You are entering a sunny playground, surrounded by tall, strong trees. Take a deep, long breath in. You notice this playground smells of the fresh mulch underfoot and the grass surrounding the playground that must've been very recently cut. It reminds you of happy summer memories.

You step towards the swing set and notice it is the tallest swing set you've ever seen! Wow! Look at how tall this swing set is and how high this swing must be able to swing! You love to swing and know you want to try it out for yourself right away.

You hop on the giant swing and settle yourself into the comfortable, flexible rubber seat warm from being kissed by the summer sun. It is the most comfortable swing you have ever been on, and you shimmy back and forth as you get yourself positioned in the perfect spot.

This swing has the softest rubber grips to hold on to, and you squeeze them in your hands a little. Everything about this swing set is perfect! You begin to kick your feet back and forth, back and forth, just very gently at first, your hands firmly holding on to the rubber grips.

Because this swing set is so tall, it feels like it takes a lot more work to get yourself going, but you don't mind because it feels good to stretch your legs out in front and bring them back again as you pump back and forth, back and forth. Your whole body is getting into it now, and this swing is getting going.

A warm summer breeze blows through the playground, and you watch the leaves on the trees flutter back and forth. You can hear the birds singing their summer songs in the trees. You take a deep breath in and think you can smell somewhere in the distance, someone firing up a grill for a barbecue. Wow, what a perfect summer day!

You continue to pump your legs back and forth, back and forth. The blood is pumping in your legs now, and your muscles feel great from the workout! You notice how high you are swinging now! Wow! You feel as if you are almost as high as the treetops that surround you!

You look up at the bright blue sky overhead. It is a beautiful summer day, and the sun is now behind you, so you can see the clear blue sky and the fluffy white clouds in the distance perfectly. You keep swinging, higher, and higher still.

It almost feels as if you could swing right into the sky, you are swinging so high now! The summer breeze is warm and light, and you close your eyes for a moment to enjoy the sensation of the light breeze as it caresses your face. You take in another long, deep breath and smell the fresh pine mulch below mixing in with the other scents of summer, the fresh-cut grass all around you and the barbeque in the distance.

You are so happy as you continue to swing back and forth, back and forth, listening to the cheerful chirping of the birds in the trees around you. Your legs are strong and keep you swinging higher and higher, and your hands are perfectly comfortable as they continue to firmly hold on to the rubber grips. You love the way the muscles on your legs and arms feel as they warm up. You realize you have a huge, happy grin on your face because you are so happy.

You open your eyes back up and see that you are swinging higher than the treetops around you! Wow! You are swinging so high now it almost feels as if you are flying through the air, and you think that this must be the way it feels to be a bird soaring on the breeze.

You fly through the air, back and forth, back and forth, feeling 100% happy and contented. Everything is perfect at this moment right now, and you let your eyes drink in the deep blue of the sky as you swing so high it feels as if you are swinging out in the wide-open summer sky. You are so grateful to be experiencing this wonderful summer day.

You do not have to stop swinging right now if you don't want to. You can keep swinging into the beautiful clear blue summer sky just as long as you want to, and you can come back here anytime you'd like.

You can create anything you want in your mind. Imagine where you want to go and build the picture in your mind. Be sure to imagine how you want it to smell, taste, hear, and feel. The more detailed you can make your mental picture, the more you will enjoy being there.

It is all up to you. Perhaps as you drift off to sleep, you will find yourself back in your giant swing, swinging yourself into a blue summer sky.

Tyrannosaurus

Teri was born high up on a hillside in a little town called Kingstown. Her Momma was one of the biggest T Rex's in the whole town, and everyone knew to be polite to her because she was one of the town's leaders. When Teri was born, she was the last one to peck her way out of her egg, which made her the runt of the litter. Terri did have 4 big brothers, but they were too rough with her, and she usually had to hide under her mother's huge body when things got a little out of hand.

Because Teri was the runt of the litter, she had to try extra hard in school and had a hard time making friends. You see, her big brothers had gone around and told all the other children that little Teri was a runt and wasn't worth talking to. Teri didn't like that, but she knew that it would be up to her to do something about it, so that is exactly what she did.

Teri remembered when she and her brothers were toddlers, and Mom used to teach them all about how to be good kids and get along with the others. She always said that if you take the time to smell the roses, you will always have a clear mind and a strong will. Teri remembered that her Momma called it mindfulness, and she said it went hand in hand with something called meditation.

Med-it-ta-shon!

She remembered that she had some trouble pronouncing that word when she first heard it, but after she learned what meditation was, she was thrilled. Her brothers, not so much. All they wanted to do was play-fight and horse around.

Now that Teri was no longer a toddler and was becoming a nice little girl, she had a great idea! What if I could teach some of the other kid's meditation? Then, "I" would be the teacher, and the teacher always got a lot of attention. Teri liked that idea because right now, no one ever noticed her, and she was feeling very lonely and left out.

That evening after school, she rushed home and dug out the book, her Momma had given the children when they were first hatched. It was called "Tranquility." She opened it up, and some dust fell out and had a nasty musty smell. "Pewffff!" she uttered as the dust cloud finally drifted away. "I guess it has been a while," Teri said as she held the old book up and shook the pages just to make sure nothing was hiding in there. Soon she settled back against an old Oak tree near their house and began reading. She read, and she read, and she didn't notice that it was getting dark out, and she was not supposed to be out after dark. Her Momma had made that real clear several times already, so she panicked and grabbed up her book and hurried inside.

"Where have you been, child?" her Momma snapped. "I was just right outside Momma reading this," she said, holding up the old book so her Momma could see it. "Why that's wonderful," her Momma said lovingly. Teri was surprised that Momma could change her mood so quickly over a silly old book. But maybe it wasn't a silly old book. Yes! That must be it. Teri knew she was on the right track right then because she was able to turn her Momma's scorn into praise with just the sight of this dirty old book. When little Teri went to bed that night, she fell asleep with a smile on her pretty little face. She had a plan!

The next morning at the Kingstown School, the teacher asked that everyone share something of interest that they did over the weekend. Teri was twitching with excitement, and some of the other kids were giving her funny looks. When it was her turn to share, she got up in front of her class and began. "Mindfulness!" she said. And then smiled big. The teacher cleared her throat, and about half the class started to laugh. That is until she spoke again.

"Mindfulness and meditation can bring us closer together because closer together is how we are supposed to be," Teri said with authority. She reveled in her newfound confidence as she spoke. "Mindfulness is peacefulness, and peacefulness is how we all love each other and get along better." She continued, "We all have to breathe, we all have to see, and we all have to smell the flowers when the flowers are smelly!" she stated. Teri liked this new feeling of child power; she felt rumbling through her little body. All of the lessons from the day's way back when she and her brothers were just toddlers came tumbling back into her mind. She remembered everything her Momma had taught them.

"So, with that in mind, I would like to ask our teacher for her permission, and if she will give it, I would like to invite all of you to a kid group I am starting. It will be called Mindfulness and Meditation for us!"

The teacher was beaming the biggest smile Teri had ever seen her smile, and the kids exploded into applause. She got everyone's attention in the class. Did this mean she was no longer the runt? It sure seemed that way to her. In the next few days, most of the class wanted to know more about meditation. What was it? how did it work? and what was it for? Teri's Momma set up a place in the family garage so the kids could all meet there, and since it was summer, they left the big garage door open so the cool summer breeze could come wafting in .

Teri read aloud from the book. "A mindful individual is peaceful. Mindfulness in adults is about noticing everything in their environment. Mindfulness in children is about being polite and well natured and about respecting their parents and others around them. We, as children, should get a jump on life by meditating.

Beginning with their breathing, an essential force of life, and moving outwards in an ever-increasing circle. Noticing our emotions as well as the task at hand is the key. Mindful children are friendly children who easily attract friends or others who they do not even know. The attraction comes from the sense of wellbeing and confidence a mindful child cannot help but to radiate."

Then, Teri's Momma came out into the garage with a huge tray of cookies and milk. "Hooray!" yelled all the children and jumped up to get their refreshments.

The years passed by, and the Kingstown Kids all started to grow up. Most of them stayed in touch with each other because they all felt a bond together and that bond was started right there in that summer garage with cookies and milk and little Teri and her little book called "Tranquility!"

So, Teri solved the problem of being called the runt and made lots of new friends. She was also the one who helped all the other kids in her class become very good friends, and those friends, every one of them went on to be successful in their lives. Some became doctors, some became lawyers, and some became business executives, but all used mindfulness and meditation to climb to the top of the world. You can be like Teri too. Just go looking for a dusty old little book with the name of "Tranquility."

The Buffaloes

Once upon a time, four big buffaloes used to live deep in the forest. They always did everything together: they ate together, they played together and they slept together. They were so close that all the other animals were afraid of them. Among those animals, there was a tiger. Every time he planned to attack them, they were together, so he always had to abandon his plan. They were four and the tiger was just one, so the buffaloes were stronger:

- Oh, how will I attack them if they´re always together? Never mind! I will try again tomorrow. – the disappointed tiger would say to himself.

One day, the four friends made a plan:

- Listen! I was told the other day that the grass on the other side of the fence is greener. Why don't we go there for lunch now and see if it's true? – suggested one of the buffaloes.

- Oh, yes! Why not? Let's stop chatting. Let´s go. – said another buffalo.

- Hmm, green grass. My mouth is watering already just thinking about it. – said, yet, another one.

- Ha, ha, ha ... you hungry bison! Will you ever stop thinking about food, Fatso? – said one of the buffaloes laughing at him.

They all left together to check out the lawn and as they walked ahead, a fox saw them coming, but she was so scared of them that she immediately ran away. The four buffaloes did not even notice her; they walked merrily along the path, thinking about the green grass they were going to munch on and didn't pay attention to anything else.

After a while, they were able to get to the lawn on the other side of the fence. After walking for so long, they all were tired and hungry. As they were about to start eating, one of them said:

- Let's do something. Why don't we let Fatso watch over us while we are eating? – said one of the buffaloes.

- But, that is not fair! Why should I have to wait longer than you? I am starving too! – said the very hungry buffalo.

- You take longer to eat. You can eat after us while we watch over you. - said another buffalo.

- I still think it isn't fair. I am not your servant. I will not wait and watch over you while you eat. I will be eating with you. – replied the hungry and hurt buffalo.

- He´s right! It isn´t fair to make him wait alone here. We´re all starving. – said, yet, another one.

- Really? So, why don't you wait while Fatso comes and eats with us? – replied one of the other buffaloes

- Who do you think you are? You can't boss us around like that. - replied the hungry bison, crossly.

- Well, if I bother you so much, I will leave right away. You have always bossed me around in the past and I have never complained about it. – replied the buffalo.

- Yeah, you boss us around all the time. – replied the hungry bison.

- Yeah, I will leave too. I do not need any of you. I can be on my own. – said, yet, another one.

- Yeah, I can be on my own too. Go away, all of you. – replied the hungry and angry bison.

All four of them were getting mad at each other and they did not notice that the tiger had followed them there and was watching. The tiger had dreamt day and night about this moment. He always hoped that the four of them would get into a really big fight.

After fighting, the four buffaloes went off in different directions. This was a perfect time for the tiger to attack:

- I cannot believe my eyes. My lucky day has finally arrived. Now I can attack and eat them one by one. – said the tiger, happily.

- The four friends walked away from each other. The tiger followed and jumped on them one after another. He killed and ate all of them.

While the four buffaloes were together no one ever dared to go near them, but after fighting and leaving each other, they lost their lives.

As they say: "Unity is our greatest strength".

The Magician

Have you been to a magic show? Better yet, have you been a component of a magic show? What in case I told you you may be a component of a magic show right away if you ever needed to? You can! You really can- In the mind of yours! Your mind can do many great things, which includes a thing known as Visualization.

To begin your visualization practice, close your eyes. Close your eyes (unless you are the one reading this, of course!) To build a very strong visualization, it is usually helpful to first center yourself and be sure you are giving your brain the very best tools it needs to work with. In this case, that means oxygen, and oxygen means taking some good, deep breaths .

You are going to take some slow, deep breaths now, following my instruction: Breathe in very slowly, 1 – 2 – 3 – 4. Now breathe out, very slowly, 1 – 2 – 3 – 4. Excellent. Now again very slowly, 1 – 2 – 3 – 4 and breathe back out very slowly, 1 – 2 – 3 – 4 very nice. Once more, very slowly in 1 – 2 – 3 – 4 and back out very slowly, 1 – 2 – 3 – 4. Great!

Take a moment to review how you feel. Are you comfy and feeling good? Okay, great.

Imagine yourself, in your mind's eye, in an audience in a huge, dimly lit auditorium. Looking around you, you can see this place is packed! Up on stage, there is a spotlight and one standing front and center with a small table in front of him and a single chair next to the table. Look closer, who is that person?

He is very tall with black hair, and he appears to have some sort of a cape and top hat on. He takes the top hat off and looks to be rummaging around within the hat... how deep is that thing anyway! It looks like his whole arm is in his hat! And what on earth is he pulling out of it now? Oh, my goodness, look! It's a fluffy white bunny rabbit!

You and the rest of the audience applaud this amazing trick. How cool! This person is a magician, and you are at a magic show. Wow! Take a moment and take a long, deep breath in. You can smell the old auditorium with its worn leather seats and its maple wood stage. Just then, you hear the magician asking the crowd for a volunteer to come up on stage.

You have never been on stage as a magician's volunteer before, and you have to think a moment; what do you think the magician will need the volunteer to do? Will you be nervous? You realize your arm is already going up as you are thinking through it all because your excitement wins out over your worry every time. Now the magician is looking directly at you and motioning for you to come up! Wow! This is incredible!

You get up and out of your seat and make y our way out of your row. The other audience members are congratulating you on being picked. Everyone is very excited to see what will happen next, including you! ou can feel the pleasure in the ambiance as you create the solution of yours up the actions onto the point.

The magician welcomes you up on the stage and asks you to sit on the chair beside the table. You take a seat, and he immediately hands you the fluffy white bunny that he had just pulled from his hat. He tells you his bunny's name is Fluffy and that it is your job to keep

Fluffy comfortable during this next trick, so you will need to pet Fluffy and keep her calm.

The magician reaches back into his top hat and begins rummaging around again. Oh, my goodness, seriously. How deep is that thing? He pulls out a large blueish black velvet drape and brings it over to where you are sitting with Fluffy. You are petting Fluffy and smiling. Fluffy's fur is so soft, and the lights of the stage are so warm as you sit petting this fluffy white bunny rabbit.

The magician drapes the bluish-black velvet drape over you and Fluffy and reminds you that you must keep petting Fluffy and keep her comfortable during this next trick. You are feeling so excited now to see what this trick will be! The magician takes his wand and waves it around both you and Fluffy a few times and says some silly magic words and voila!

The magician pulls the drape off of you and Fluffy bunny in one swift motion, revealing that instead of Fluffy Bunny in your lap, you are now holding and petting a stuffed bunny rabbit toy! You and the audience gasp together.

Your mouth drops open in disbelief, how did this happen? What on earth is going on? Where is the little fluffy bunny rabbit you had been petting? The magician motions to your head, and you reach up to feel that you are now wearing the magician's tall top hat on your very own head. You pull the top hat off and guess what's underneath? Fluffy Bunny Rabbit!!!!

The audience erupts into applause as the magician scoops the fluffy bunny rabbit up off of your head and returns him to the table with the tall top hat. The magician motions for you to stand up and take a bow as he thanks you for your assistance. You are still in absolute disbelief on how on earth he did this trick when he tells you that you can keep stuffed bunny rabbit toy as a souvenir .

You make your way back off the stage and to your seat, with the other audience members clapping for you and the magician. Once you've sat back down on the cool leather seat, you realize you are grinning ear to ear. You are so happy to be a part of this magic show, and you know that it has been an experience that you will never forget. Plus, you have this soft fluffy bunny rabbit toy to always help you remember it by. You feel so thankful that you have had this incredibly cool magic show experience!

You do not have to leave this magic show just yet if you don't want to. You can stay here in the audience, watching these amazing magic tricks as long as you want, and you can come back here anytime you'd like.

You can create anything you want in your mind. Imagine where you want to go and build the picture in your mind. Be sure to imagine how you want it to smell, taste, hear, and feel. The greater comprehensive you can make the mental picture of yours, the more you'll enjoy being there.

It is all up to you. Perhaps as you drift off to sleep, you may find yourself back here in the auditorium with the maple wood stage, waiting for the magician to ask for another volunteer from the audience.

The Great Unicorn Hunter

Minash's father had been chief of the tribe his entire life. Ever since he was a little boy, his father had been the one man in the tribe that everyone looked to and watched. He liked his father, but sometimes it was a little tiresome to be the great leader's son. Sometimes he just wanted to be a boy, like other boys, and hunt and fish without everyone always watching him, wondering if he was going to be chief someday.

But that all changed when the great chief had suddenly died in the hot season. Nobody had expected him to be carried off by the great spirit so soon. His mother, Junebug, had been so sad. But it hadn't kept her from pushing him forward as the next leader. Yes, he was still a sapling, but he was growing stronger and who better to lead the tribe in the time going forward but the son of the great leader.

Other, older braves were perhaps readier than he was. But, Junebug had argued at the last council, are they fallen from the same tree as Minash? As summers come and go, will they be able to lead? Is it in their blood? The summer end hunt was going to be important, she'd told him when they were alone. Whichever of the braves brought back the finest catch would be the next leader, she told him. In these matters, she was seldom wrong.

That night, when he was praying to his spirit guide, he was told the answer. It was the path he was sure his father would have wanted him to take. He would be the first of his tribe to capture a unicorn and bring it back alive. Many stories had been told about the great animal, the unicorn. Some said it could never be killed, immortal, and would simply vanish away when struck by arrow or spear. Both Minash and his father had spoken of the creature. They both believed it could not be killed. Which is why nobody had ever eaten one.

But they both did believe it existed and could be captured and caged. The ancients had claimed once there was one who had done so. And that was the origin of their tribe. When captured, the unicorn's magical powers go to the tribe who have done so.

Minash would capture the unicorn and bring honor to his family and tribe. Like his father, he would be a great leader. This he told his mother that very night. She then gave him the rope she said was magical. When placed over the unicorn, it would obey. This bridle was said to have been woven with strands from the very bridle that had once captured the unicorn in the tribe's beginning .

The men set off early the following morning. The sun wasn't yet up and they all went to the fantastic forest, beyond the river. They will travel together until the forest, then hunt on their paths deep into the forest. Minash had gone with the father of his many times and knew the forest well. There were many fierce and strange creatures, though none more elusive compared to the unicorn. After, his dad had seen a glimpse of one, by a stream. Which was where Dorian would go.

The braves walked together that day, and they joked among themselves who was the greatest hunter. They were careful not to joke too carelessly about Minash, though. Perhaps it was because they thought him too young, and not a threat. But maybe, Minash thought, it was something else. They were always careful with his father too. When they came to the forest, they camped together one last time. Each brave offered prayers and they ate some food they had brought and sat by a fire. It would be the last food many of them would eat. In five days they would meet there again and then return to the village.

Before it was light the next morning Minash left, saying nothing to the still sleeping braves. He went into the forest alone, and he found his path. He was full of some energy he'd never known before. Or maybe he'd never felt it so strongly. He felt the spirit guide was with him and this made him feel strong and invincible .

The forest was thick and sounds were forest sounds. The howl of monkeys far off, the cackle of unseen birds far up in the trees. Minash found the stream he was looking for. He would follow it for half a day, then come to the place where it pooled out, then tightened into a small waterfall. That was where his father had seen the unicorn. Minash would wait there in a tree above the waterfall. The unicorn would show itself then he would catch it with the rope. The other braves would be looking to spear lions or great monkeys. He would capture the unicorn.

When he came to the pool and the waterfall, Minash drank long. He knew he might be days in the tree. Minash climbed into the tree and waited. After some time, animals began to appear to drink at the pool. Small birds and some deer. Spots of sun would appear here and there, as the trees bent a little in the breezes above. Two boars came by. As it became dark, a lion came to the pool and quietly lapped at the water. No unicorn appeared the first day.

Nor did one come the second or third day, though other animals came to drink. Some, so strange. Monkeys with bright colors. An animal like a lion, but entirely black. Minash quickly thought the black lion would have been a good prize to bring to the village, but then resisted the urge to reach for an arrow.

On the fourth day, though, as Minash hung up in the trees, tired and thirsty, thinking even to steal down for a drink, his heart suddenly quickened. He spied some white form among the lower trees. Then, a quick glimpse of something hard and shiny came out from the trees for a moment. Minash thought surely this was the unicorn, needing a drink perhaps, but being careful. He held himself still. He thought to himself breath as quietly as possible. Do not move even the smallest movement. Minash thought to pray to the spirit that he might be worthy to capture such an animal. He vowed, that if this was allowed, he would be a wise, just and generous leader. This was the most solemn vow he'd ever made. He knew, somehow, in the spirit world, his father would hear it and be proud of his son.

Just then the unicorn emerged from the trees. It had a magnificent white coat, the purest coat he'd ever seen. The horn seemed to pierce the sky itself. The animal came to just before the waterfall, where his father had said he'd seen it before. The unicorn walked proudly and gracefully, then as it went to lower its muzzle into the water below him, Minash dropped the rope over its neck and pulled back instantly to tighten it. The unicorn reared back, but it was too late, he was captured.

Minash leaped down from the tree with the rope in his hand and stood next to the captured unicorn. He was filled with wonder and awe at its beauty. The unicorn seemed to know it was captured and did not resist. It seemed even to relax as it watched its new master. Minash was filled with the same peace he remembered feeling when he was hunting with his father. Rather than shout out in victory, Minash felt only humility and then gratitude that such a magnificent beast existed in the same world he did.

With the unicorn close by on the rope, Minash went back to the village and was made leader at the next council. Minash would lead his tribe through many years of great peace and prosperity.

True greatness is born from humility.

Sleep time: You're going to sleep in a great forest tonight, where the unicorn lives. What are the sounds you hear?

Ilongoria

Jennifer Bradley wanted to be a princess. Sure, she was only nine years old and had already received a glittering tiara for her head and a red velvet cape to adorn her beautiful little shoulders, but she knew that this was just make-believe. Toys that her parents had given her for birthdays. She wanted to be a real princess, a real, true life princess with a castle and her own thrown to sit upon as she ruled the land. Jennifer Bradley wanted to be a princess more than anything else in the world.

Jennifer had a best friend in school who had told her about meditation, and she had begun to practice this wonderful pastime. She felt so good when she was meditating because she was raising her vibration to a higher level. She had not figured this out yet, but at such a young age, this would take some time.

Jennifer's parents were highly intelligent and compassionate people and understood the importance of meditation and mindfulness.

They talked to her about this and made certain that any problems or questions she had could be brought to them at any time and that they would support her.

Jennifer believed that her life was special. She began to meditate right before going to bed every night, and this, she thought, was creating something in her little life that she did not expect. One night, she had what she thought was a dream. In the morning, she sat up and thought, "That felt so real. I remember every detail and every face of every person in that dream." And then she got up and went down to breakfast, and off to school like any other day.

But, all day, she could not get her mind off that dream. She was not focusing on her studies, and that was not like her. Even the teachers noticed and thought that she was just starting to daydream, which would have been way out of character for her.

On the following night, to her great surprise, she returned to the very same dream. But this time, it was real! "Miss Ilongoria, welcome back to the kingdom," a voice said behind her. She turned and found herself staring at a young man dressed in medieval clothing right down to the funny hat and the round collar. "What did you call me?" she asked. "Your Royal Highness," he said, bowing slightly, "I understand you may be perplexed; however, you are here now, and you are the chosen one, you are Princess Ilongoria. It has always been so. You are the young princess who has been prophesied to be the one."

Jennifer gulped. While it was true that she had wanted to be a princess for the entirety of her short life, this was a stunning surprise. Perhaps this was why she wanted to be a princess, because she was destined to be one. "No, that can't be true?" she puzzled. "You can't just be something because you want to be? Or can you?" just then, the strange man spoke again.

"I feel an explanation is in order." He stated. "Come over here, child, and take this seat." He said, pointing to what looked to Jennifer, just like a small throne. She followed his lead and sat down. The chair was extremely comfortable and was handmade by craftsmen. This she could tell. The seat and back-rest were quite puffy and were a red velvet material but much softer and deeper to sit upon than they appeared. The wood of the back frame, handpieces, and legs was a very deep and dark brown color, and both the feet and the handpieces were eagles claws grasping a large round ball.

"This room is a special place. This is where we both welcome and bid farewell to those who come and go to and from other lands, other dimensions if you will." Jennifer gasped. "You were born to be Princess Ilongoria, and your parents know this. In your life on Earth, it would have been problematic to inform you of such things, but now you have reached the proper age and can begin to learn of your true destiny." He sat down in a chair across from her and continued. "I am the king's Royal Council, and I have been charged with assisting you in your transformation. Whatever you need, whatever you desire, I shall produce." He stated .

"But now we must make haste. The King and Queen of Ilongoria await your arrival, and you must change. I will leave this chamber and allow you your privacy to do so." He walked over to a huge mirrored armoire and opened the big door revealing the finest of gowns and robes she had ever seen. You must adorn yourself it these." He said, pulling out an emerald green outfit that looked beautiful to her.

"When you are ready, simply say, "I am ready, squire." And I shall return for you." He told her and left the room. She quickly slipped into the gorgeous attire and then said the words. The Royal Counsel returned and escorted her out and down a long hall. Then up a long flight of stairs that went back and forth as it rose. Finally, they arrived on a landing overlooking a massive hall that looked like a church to her. Then, they stopped walking, and the Counsel turned to face her.

We have arrived at the Royal Chamber, and these doors are always open to you. You should feel like you are home when you are here. After we enter, we shall both walk down the red carpet leading to the Royal Thrones, and we shall stop before their Royal Highnesses. At that point, you must curtsy and await their greeting. Is that clear? The Counsel said.

"Yes, I understand," Jennifer stated, wondering if was even Jennifer any longer. Did she have some kind of royal first name that was fit for a princess?" she thought. "We shall soon find out." She mused. The Council opened the tall double doors, and they walked, side-by-side into the Royal Chamber.

When Jennifer saw the King and Queen, she was stunned. They looked like her real Mother and Father. "How can this be?" she thought. The King stood up and stepped down off the landing towards her. "Princess Ilongoria!" He said in a deep kingly voice. "We have awaited the honor of your presence for some time now. We are so very pleased that you have reached the age and can now take your place beside us on your throne." The king stated.

He held out his hand, and when she touched it, she felt a bolt of energy, and she was certain she had seen a blue flash at his fingertips. He took her hand and led her over to a throne that was to the right of the king's great throne. In this way, he had the Queen on his left, and his Princess on his right side. As she sat, a bright flash engulfed her, and she was back in her bed at home. She noticed the sun streaming through her open window and realized that morning had come to her town and that it was time for breakfast and then school again.

She got up and did the usual morning routine of her then went down the stairs to breakfast. She smelled bacon and knew that her Momma was in the kitchen, making her family another wonderful morning meal. She entered the kitchen and saw her father sitting at the table, reading the morning paper. He dropped the paper down onto the table and looked up at her. " Did you enjoy your visit to Dorian last night, little one?" He said. She stopped and stared at him with big eyes. "Dorian?" was all she could say at the moment. "Yes, child," her Momma chimed in. "Dorian is the realm of the King and Queen of Orange. You are their princess. You must know that by now, dear, now come sit down and enjoy your bacon and eggs. We have pancakes too, so I hope you are hungry this morning, little one." She said calmly.

Jennifer had so many questions in her head but chose to just play along. She had matured in the past few weeks to the point of knowing that being mindful and keeping up her meditation was the key to everything that was happening and that her role in this part of her life was to teach the other children the unseen powers of mindfulness. "Pass the syrup please, Father?" she asked.

Meditation is the key.

www.ingramcontent.com/pod-product-compliance
Lightning Source LLC
Chambersburg PA
CBHW070857080526
44589CB00027B/1497